One-Pot Wonders

Woman's Day

One-Pot Wonders

Effortless meals for hectic nights

filipacchi publishing

Filipacchi Publishing
1633 Broadway
New York, NY 10019

© 2003 Filipacchi Publishing
Cover photograph © Jacqueline Hopkins

Designed by Patricia Fabricant
Copyedited by Margaret Farley, Greg Robertson and
Kim Walker

ISBN 2-85018-782-8

Printed and bound in Italy

Contents

Take one pot, fill it with something you crave, turn on the heat and don't worry—you'll be happy! That's the magic behind *Woman's Day*'s *One-Pot Wonders*, which serves up 58 easy answers to the question, "What's for dinner?" Find a solution, whether you need to get something on the table quick, quick, quick, or you want to turn on the slow-cooker and go, go, go. Just assemble the ingredients and let the casserole dish, skillet or pot do the work. Any woman in a hurry to get things done—and who isn't these days?—will appreciate these simple but satisfying recipes that practically cook themselves. How convenient!

These dishes go far beyond one bland, boring food item on a plate: They're complete, hearty meals, including servings of fruits, vegetables and grains, done with 21st century ease. Many of the ingredients are staples you probably already have in your pantry, refrigerator or freezer. Are you crazy about chicken or do you have a palate for pork? We've got you covered. Need a vegetarian meal or something with seafood? No problem! Tempting tastes of lamb, turkey, beef—they're in here. Enjoy everything from stews and stir fries to pasta and paella, all in easy-to-follow recipes cooked on top of the stove or baked in the oven. Whether you're looking for a recipe with an Asian influence, an Italian entrée or an all-American favorite, you're sure to find meals that will please everyone in your family, even the pickiest eaters.

Think no stress, and very little mess to clean up afterward. Who knows, your kids may even volunteer to do the dishes on one-pot nights.

Fast cook, slow cook, anyway you cook it, just turn out a meal from *One-Pot Wonders* and relax!

Balsamic Chicken with Thyme

1/4 cup flour
3/4 tsp each *salt and freshly ground pepper*
4 *skinless, boneless chicken-breast halves (about 5 oz each)*
2 Tbsp olive oil
1 *large red onion, cut in half lengthwise, then thinly sliced (2 cups)*
About 1 cup chicken broth
2 Tbsp balsamic vinegar
2 tsp fresh thyme leaves or 1/2 tsp dried

1 Mix flour and 1/2 tsp *each* salt and pepper on a plate. Add chicken; turn to coat. Shake off excess.

2 In a large cast-iron or other heavy skillet, heat oil over medium heat. Add chicken and cook, turning once, 10 minutes or until browned and cooked through. Remove to a plate; cover to keep warm.

3 Add onion to skillet and sauté 1 to 2 minutes until lightly browned. Add broth, vinegar, thyme and remaining 1/4 tsp *each* salt and pepper. Bring to a boil and cook, stirring often, 7 minutes or until onions are soft (see Tip) and sauce is syrupy.

4 Place chicken on plates; spoon on onions and sauce.

TIME: 37 min

SERVES 4

PER SERVING: 286 cal,
35 g pro, 14 g car, 2 g fiber,
9 g fat (2 g saturated fat),
82 mg chol, 787 mg sod

TIP *If the onion isn't soft after cooking 7 minutes (Step 3), add a little more broth and continue cooking until it is.*

TIME: 1 hr 10 min

SERVES 6

PER SERVING: 434 cal,
  36 g pro, 39 g car, 3 g fiber,
  14 g fat (3 g saturated fat),
  127 mg chol, 993 mg sod

TIP *Use kitchen scissors to snip off any visible fat from the raw thighs.*

PARSLEY DUMPLINGS

1 1/3 cups flour
2 tsp baking powder
1/4 tsp salt
2 Tbsp minced fresh
  flat-leaf parsley
3/4 cup plus 1 Tbsp 1%
  lowfat milk

In a medium bowl, stir flour, baking powder and salt to mix. Stir in parsley, then milk just until blended.

Texas Chicken and Dumplings

2 lb skinless, boneless chicken thighs (see Tip)
1/4 cup flour
3/4 tsp each salt and freshly ground pepper
3 Tbsp vegetable oil
1 leek (white part only), thinly sliced, rinsed and dried
1/4 cup minced shallots or onion
1 1/2 cups chicken broth
2 slender carrots, cut diagonally in 1/4-in.-wide slices
2 celery stalks, cut in 1/4-in. dice
1/2 cup apple cider or juice
1 bay leaf
2 tsp chopped fresh thyme, or 1/2 tsp dried
1 tsp minced fresh sage, or 1/4 tsp dried
1/2 cup frozen tiny peas

1 Cut each thigh lengthwise in 4 pieces. Mix flour and 1/2 tsp *each* salt and pepper on a plate. Add chicken; turn to coat. Shake off excess.

2 In a large, heavy skillet, heat oil over medium-high heat. Add chicken in batches and cook 1 minute per side or until lightly browned. Remove to a plate.

3 Add leek and shallots to skillet. Cook over medium heat 2 minutes or until soft. Return chicken; add broth, carrots, celery, cider, bay leaf, thyme, sage and remaining 1/4 tsp *each* salt and pepper. Reduce heat to medium-low, partially cover and cook, stirring occasionally, 10 minutes or until carrots and celery are crisp-tender. Stir in peas.

4 Make dumplings (see *left*). Drop 12 large spoonfuls of dumpling mixture into the simmering broth. Cook 10 minutes, cover and cook 10 minutes more or until a toothpick inserted into center of a dumpling comes out clean.

5 Discard bay leaf. Ladle chicken, vegetables, broth and dumplings into large, deep bowls.

Hunter's Chicken

1 cup uncooked orzo (rice-shaped pasta)
1 Tbsp oil, preferably olive
10 oz mushrooms, sliced (see Tip)
1 can (28 oz) crushed tomatoes
1 red bell pepper, cut in narrow strips
1 medium onion, cut in narrow strips
1 Tbsp minced garlic
1 tsp each dried basil, oregano and salt
4 skinless, boneless oven-roaster chicken thighs (about 1 1/4 lb),
    trimmed of fat and cut in half crosswise
TOPPINGS: minced parsley, grated Parmesan cheese

1 Bring 4 cups water to boil in large nonstick skillet.
Add orzo and boil uncovered over medium-high heat, stirring occasionally, 9 minutes or until firm-tender. Drain well.

2 Heat oil in same skillet. Add mushrooms and sauté 3
to 4 minutes until lightly golden. Remove to a bowl.

3 In skillet, mix tomatoes, bell pepper, onion, garlic,
basil, oregano and salt. Add chicken thighs and bring to a
boil; reduce heat, cover and simmer 5 minutes, stirring
once. Stir in orzo, cover and cook 6 minutes longer or
until chicken is cooked through. Stir in mushrooms; sprinkle with parsley and cheese.

TIME: 37 min

SERVES 4

PER SERVING: 441 cal,
    38 g pro, 50 g car, 5 g fiber,
    10 g fat (2 g saturated fat),
    118 mg chol, 1,036 mg sod

TIP Cut up the vegetables
while the orzo cooks.

TIME: 30 min

SERVES 4

PER SERVING: 415 cal, 35 g pro,
41 g car, 5 g fiber, 13 g fat
(2 g saturated fat), 94 mg
chol, 757 mg sod

TIP *To remove skin from drumsticks, grasp skin firmly with a paper towel and pull it off.*

African Chicken Stew

8 chicken drumsticks (about 2 lb), skin removed (see Tip)
1/8 tsp each salt and pepper
2 medium sweet potatoes
2 tsp minced garlic
1 tsp chili powder
1 can (14 1/2 oz) diced tomatoes with garlic and onion
1 cup frozen green peas
1/3 cup each reduced-fat crunchy peanut butter and water
1 Tbsp lemon juice

1 Season chicken with salt and pepper. Coat a nonstick 10- or 12-in. skillet with nonstick cooking spray. Place over medium-high heat, add chicken and cook 3 minutes or until browned.

2 Meanwhile peel potatoes and cut in bite-size pieces.

3 Sprinkle drumsticks with garlic and chili powder (1 side only), turn drumsticks over and cook 30 seconds until fragrant.

4 Add potatoes and tomatoes; place drumsticks on top. Bring to a boil, reduce heat, cover and simmer 10 minutes. Sprinkle with peas, cover and cook 10 minutes or until chicken is cooked through and potatoes are tender.

5 Using a slotted spoon, remove chicken to serving platter. Add remaining ingredients to skillet; stir until blended and hot. Pour over chicken.

Spaghetti with Sausage and Peppers

2 tsp oil, preferably olive

1 lb sweet Italian turkey sausage, sliced crosswise in 1-in.-wide pieces (see Tip)

1 each red and yellow bell pepper, cut in narrow strips

1 Tbsp minced garlic

4 cups water

1 tsp dried basil

2 chicken bouillon cubes

8 oz thin spaghetti, broken in thirds

2 1/2 cups frozen cut-leaf spinach

GARNISH: Parmesan cheese shaved off a chunk with a vegetable peeler

1 Heat oil in a large nonstick skillet over medium-high heat. Add sausage, peppers and garlic. Sauté 3 to 4 minutes until peppers are crisp-tender.

2 Add water, basil and bouillon cubes. Bring to a boil. Stir spaghetti into liquid. Gently boil, uncovered, until pasta is limp, about 5 minutes.

3 Stir in spinach, cover, reduce heat and simmer 4 minutes. Uncover, increase heat and boil gently 6 to 8 minutes, stirring often until spaghetti is firm-tender and liquid is nearly absorbed but mixture is still saucy. Serve garnished with Parmesan cheese.

TIME: 30 min

SERVES 4

PER SERVING: 469 cal, 31 g pro, 54 g car, 5 g fiber, 16 g fat (4 g saturated fat), 61 mg chol, 1,327 mg sod

TIP Freeze the sausage 20 minutes to make slicing easier.

Sausage and Potato Frittata

4 tsp vegetable oil
1 lb lean sweet Italian turkey sausage, casing removed
1 medium zucchini (about 6 oz), thinly sliced
8 large eggs
1 can (14 1/2 oz) sliced potatoes
1 can (8 3/4 oz) corn kernels
4 oz (half an 8-oz brick) 1/3-less-fat cream cheese (Neufchâtel), diced

1 Heat 2 tsp oil in a nonstick 10-in. skillet over medium-high heat. Add sausage and zucchini. Cook, stirring and breaking up sausage with a wooden spoon, 5 to 6 minutes until sausage is cooked through and zucchini is tender. Let cool.

2 Meanwhile whisk eggs in a medium bowl, and drain the potatoes and corn. Stir sausage, zucchini, potatoes and corn into eggs, then stir in cream cheese. Wipe skillet clean.

3 Heat broiler (see Note). Heat remaining 2 tsp oil in skillet over medium-low heat, tilting skillet to coat bottom and halfway up sides.

4 Add egg mixture, cover and cook 12 minutes or until eggs are set on bottom. Slide under broiler and cook just until eggs have set on top.

Skillet Chicken Parmesan with Crisp Polenta

1 large egg
1/3 cup seasoned dried bread crumbs
4 skinless, boneless chicken-breast halves (about 4 oz each)
2 Tbsp olive oil
1 tube (about 16 oz) polenta, cut in 12 slices
1/2 cup packaged shredded mozzarella with Parmesan cheese
1 1/2 cups bottled marinara sauce
GARNISH: chopped fresh basil or parsley

1 Lightly beat egg in a shallow dish. Spread crumbs on a sheet of wax paper. Dip breasts in egg, then crumbs to coat.

2 Heat 1 Tbsp oil in a large nonstick skillet over medium-high heat. Add chicken; cook 3 to 4 minutes per side or until golden and cooked through. Remove to a serving platter.

3 Wipe skillet with paper towel; heat remaining 1 Tbsp oil. Add polenta; cook 3 minutes until bottoms of slices are golden. Sprinkle tops with 1/4 cup cheese; turn slices over and cook 2 minutes until bottoms are golden and crisp. Add to platter.

4 Pour marinara sauce into skillet; bring to a simmer. Add chicken; sprinkle with remaining 1/4 cup cheese. Cover and cook 1 minute until cheese melts. Serve with polenta.

TIME: 20 min

SERVES 4

PER SERVING: 417 cal,
33 g pro, 33 g car, 4 g fiber,
16 g fat (4 g saturated fat),
121 mg chol, 1,232 mg sod

TIME: About 40 min

SERVES 4

PER SERVING: 497 cal,
 41 g pro, 60 g car, 4 g fiber,
 10 g fat (2 g saturated fat),
 114 mg chol, 1,032 mg sod

TIP *To remove the skin, grasp it with a paper towel and pull it off. To remove the fat, snip it off with kitchen scissors.*

Country Captain Chicken

2 Tbsp all-purpose flour
3 lb chicken, cut in 8 pieces, skin and visible fat removed (see Tip)
1 Tbsp vegetable oil
1 each medium onion and green bell pepper
1 can (14 1/2 oz) chicken broth
1 can (14 1/2 oz) diced tomatoes with roasted garlic
1/2 cup dark raisins
2 tsp curry powder
3/4 cup uncooked converted long-grain rice
GARNISH: *chopped parsley*

1 Place flour in a large plastic ziptop bag. Add chicken, seal bag and shake to coat chicken evenly.

2 Meanwhile heat oil in a large nonstick skillet over medium heat. Add chicken and cook, turning as needed, 5 minutes or until golden.

3 While chicken cooks, chop onion and green pepper. Push chicken to one side of skillet. Add onion and bell pepper to other side and sauté about 2 minutes until lightly browned. Stir in remaining ingredients except rice and bring to a boil.

4 Stir in rice, reduce heat, cover and simmer 20 minutes or until chicken is cooked through and rice is tender. Sprinkle with chopped parsley. Serve immediately.

Chicken with Vegetables and Brown Rice

2 skinless, boneless chicken-breast halves (about 5 oz each),
 cut in 1/2-in. pieces
1 can (14 1/2 oz) roasted vegetable and herb broth
1 Tbsp minced garlic
1 1/2 cups uncooked instant (10-minute) brown rice
1 bunch broccoli, broken in florets (6 cups)
1 red bell pepper, cut in narrow strips
1 yellow squash (about 8 oz), thinly sliced
1/2 cup grated Parmesan cheese
1/4 tsp ground black or white pepper

1 Bring chicken, broth and garlic to a boil in a large, deep skillet. Stir in the rice, broccoli florets, bell pepper strips and sliced squash.

2 Bring to a simmer, cover and cook 5 minutes. Remove from heat and let stand covered 5 minutes longer.

3 Stir in half the cheese and the ground pepper. Spoon into a serving dish; sprinkle with remaining 1/4 cup cheese.

TIME: 25 min

SERVES 4

PER SERVING: 327 cal,
 30 g pro, 46 g car, 8 g fiber,
 6 g fat (2 g saturated fat),
 49 mg chol, 682 mg sod

TIP To bulk up this healthy recipe and add more nutrients, stir in rinsed canned beans such as kidney, black, pinto or chickpeas when adding the rice.

TIME: 40 min

SERVES 4

PER SERVING: 387 cal,
 25 g pro, 55 g car, 5 g fiber,
 6 g fat (2 g saturated fat),
 56 mg chol, 1,386 mg sod

NOTE *This is a good way to use leftover chicken.*

TIP *Put a bottle of hot sauce on the table for those who like their Creole dishes spicy.*

Sausage and Chicken Jambalaya

1 tsp olive oil
8 oz reduced-fat kielbasa sausage, sliced
1 cup each sliced onion and bell pepper strips
1 1/4 cups each 8-vegetable juice and chicken broth
1 tsp Cajun seasoning
1 cup uncooked long-grain white rice
1 box (10 oz) frozen cut okra, thawed
1 cup shredded cooked chicken (see Note)
1/4 cup chopped parsley

1 Heat oil in large nonstick skillet. Add sausage, onion and bell pepper. Sauté 3 minutes or until kielbasa and vegetables are lightly browned. Stir in juice, broth and Cajun seasoning.

2 Bring to a boil, stir in rice, reduce heat to a gentle simmer, cover and cook 15 minutes. Stir in okra, return to a simmer, cover and cook 5 minutes or until rice and okra are tender. Stir in chicken; heat through. Remove from heat; stir in parsley.

Thai Chicken

1 Tbsp vegetable oil

4 chicken legs (2 1/2 lb), skin removed, each cut into
   drumsticks and thighs

1 each *medium onion and red bell pepper, thinly sliced*

2 tsp curry power

3/4 tsp salt

1 can (14 oz) light coconut milk (see Tip)

12 oz red-skinned potatoes, cut in 1-in. chunks

5 1/2 cups baby spinach (from a 6-oz bag)

1/3 cup each *basil and cilantro leaves, coarsely chopped*

1 Heat oil in a large nonstick skillet over medium heat.
Add chicken and cook, turning as needed, until lightly
browned. Remove to a plate.

2 Add onion, bell pepper, curry powder and salt to
skillet. Cover and cook 2 minutes. Stir in coconut milk,
potatoes, then the chicken.

3 Bring to a boil, reduce heat, cover skillet and simmer 20 minutes or until chicken is cooked through and
potatoes are tender when pierced.

4 Add spinach, a few handfuls at a time, stirring in more
as it cooks down. When wilted, stir in basil and cilantro.

TIME: 50 min

SERVES 4

PER SERVING: 371 cal,
   38 g pro, 24 g car, 9 g fiber,
   15 g fat (5 g saturated fat),
   130 mg chol, 756 mg sod

TIP *Make sure the label on
   the can says coconut milk,
   not cream of coconut or
   coconut water.*

TIME: 50 min

SERVES 4

PER SERVING: 595 cal,
41 g pro, 72 g car, 5 g fiber,
16 g fat (5 g saturated fat),
141 mg chol, 780 mg sod

TIP *Make sure the label on the can says coconut milk, not cream of coconut or coconut water.*

FYI *Good with wedges of refreshing honeydew melon and a twist of lime.*

Caribbean Chicken with Coconut Rice

1/4 cup flour
2 Tbsp curry powder
1 tsp salt
3/4 tsp pepper
6 skinless, boneless chicken thighs (1 1/2 lb), fat trimmed, cut crosswise in thirds
1 can (14 oz) light coconut milk (see Tip)
2/3 cup sweetened shredded coconut
1 Tbsp oil
1 1/4 cups uncooked parboiled (converted) white rice
2 cups shredded carrots (from a 10-oz bag)
1/4 cup golden raisins

1 Mix flour, curry powder, salt and pepper in a large, plastic ziptop bag. Add chicken, seal bag and shake to coat.

2 Shake can of coconut milk vigorously; pour into a 4-cup measure. Add water to equal 3 cups.

3 Stir coconut in a deep, large nonstick skillet over medium heat 3 minutes or until golden. Transfer to a small bowl.

4 Wipe skillet with a paper towel. Add 1/2 Tbsp oil and heat over medium-high heat. Add half the chicken and, turning once, cook 3 to 4 minutes until golden brown. Transfer to a bowl. Repeat with remaining oil and chicken (save flour mixture remaining in bag); return other half of chicken and any juices to skillet.

5 Whisk flour mixture in bag into coconut-milk mixture. Add to skillet along with the rice, carrots, raisins and all but 2 Tbsp toasted coconut. Stir to mix well.

6 Bring to a boil, reduce heat, cover and simmer, stirring 2 or 3 times, 20 to 25 minutes or until rice is tender and liquid absorbed. Sprinkle with reserved coconut.

Summer Turkey Chili

1 Tbsp olive oil
1 lb lean ground turkey
1 Tbsp minced garlic
2 1/2 tsp ground cumin
1/2 tsp each salt and pepper
1 can (14 1/2 oz) chicken broth
1 can (19 oz) black beans, rinsed
1 box (10 oz) frozen corn kernels
1/2 cup uncooked parboiled (converted) white rice
1/2 cup green salsa (salsa verde)
1 cup chopped sweet onion
1/2 cup chopped cilantro
ACCOMPANIMENTS: reduced-fat sour cream, green salsa and
   chopped cilantro

1 Heat oil in deep, large nonstick skillet over high heat. Add turkey and garlic and cook, stirring to break up meat, 3 to 4 minutes until browned. Add cumin, salt and pepper; cook, stirring, 30 seconds.

2 Stir in broth, beans, corn, rice and salsa. Bring to a boil, reduce heat, cover and simmer, stirring occasionally, 20 to 25 minutes until rice is tender.

3 Remove from heat; stir in onion and cilantro. Ladle into bowls; serve with accompaniments.

TIME: 45 min

SERVES 4

PER SERVING: 462 cal,
   30 g pro, 54 g car, 7 g fiber,
   14 g fat (3 g saturated fat),
   83 mg chol, 1,148 mg sod

TIME: 1 hr 5 min

SERVES 6

PER SERVING: 453 cal,
24 g pro, 45 g car, 4 g fiber,
19 g fat (5 g saturated fat),
47 mg chol, 1,502 mg sod

Chicken 'n' Biscuits

2 cups cubed cooked chicken
2 cups each cooked peas and sliced carrots
1 jar (15 oz) small whole onions, drained
2 cans (10 1/2 oz each) chicken gravy
1/2 cup milk
3/4 tsp poultry seasoning
6 frozen buttermilk biscuits (from a 26-oz bag)

1 Heat oven to 375°F.

2 In a shallow 2- to 2 1/2-qt baking dish mix chicken, peas, carrots, onions, chicken gravy, milk and seasoning.

3 Cover tightly; bake 30 minutes or until bubbly.

4 Place biscuits near edges of dish.

5 Bake until biscuits are done (about 25 minutes), lifting with a spatula to check doneness.

Deviled Chicken

1 can (10 3/4 oz) condensed cream of celery soup
1/3 cup finely chopped scallions
2 tsp coarse-grain mustard
2 tsp Worcestershire sauce
1 cup packaged seasoned bread crumbs
4 whole chicken legs, skin removed, drumsticks separated
  from thighs
2 Tbsp butter or margarine, melted

1 Heat oven to 450°F. Line a rimmed baking sheet with foil; grease foil.

2 In a medium bowl stir soup, scallions, mustard and Worcestershire sauce until blended. Place bread crumbs in a pie plate or shallow bowl.

3 Working with 1 piece at a time, roll chicken in soup mixture, then bread crumbs until well coated. Place in prepared pan and drizzle with butter.

4 Bake 50 minutes or until well-browned and chicken is opaque near the bone.

TIME: 1 hr

SERVES 4

PER SERVING: 379 cal,
  32 g pro, 28 g car, 15 g fat
  (6 g saturated fat),
  128 mg chol, 1,601 mg sod

TIP Great hot or cold.

SERVES 4

PER SERVING: 476 cal,
  23 g pro, 39 g car, 4 g fiber,
  25 g fat (11 g saturated fat),
  131 mg chol, 1,082 mg sod

FYI *Flavorful egg-shaped plum tomatoes are sometimes called Roma or Italian tomatoes. They're a good choice when ripe regular tomatoes are unavailable.*

Ravioli and Sausage Italiano

1 Tbsp olive oil
8 oz lean sweet Italian turkey-sausage links
1 each medium onion and large zucchini
1 cup Alfredo sauce (from a tub or jar)
1 1/4 cups water
1 pkg (9 oz) refrigerated four-cheese ravioli
3 plum tomatoes (see FYI), chopped
GARNISH: fresh basil leaves, cut in narrow strips

1 Heat oil in a large nonstick skillet over medium heat. Add sausage links and cook, turning as needed, until nicely browned and cooked through (see package for cook time). Remove sausage to a cutting board.

2 Meanwhile thinly slice onion and zucchini. Add to oil remaining in skillet and cook, stirring occasionally, 3 to 4 minutes until lightly browned.

3 Add Alfredo sauce and water, and stir to scrape up any browned drippings on bottom of skillet. Slice sausage in bite-size pieces.

4 Bring sauce to a boil, push ravioli under sauce, then scatter sausage and tomatoes on top. Reduce heat, cover and simmer, stirring once or twice, 8 minutes or until ravioli are tender. Sprinkle with basil; serve immediately.

Braised Pot Roast with Apricots and Prunes

One 4-lb boneless beef chuck roast
3 Tbsp all-purpose flour
4 large onions, halved lengthwise, sliced crosswise (4 cups)
3/4 tsp salt
1/2 cup each loosely packed dried apricots and pitted prunes
1 cup canned beef broth
2 tsp freshly grated lemon peel
2 Tbsp fresh lemon juice
1 tsp each minced garlic and ground cumin
1/2 tsp each ground cinnamon, ginger and pepper

1 Heat oven to 325°F.

2 Coat beef with flour; shake off excess. Put onions in a well-greased 4-qt Dutch oven. Place beef on onions and sprinkle with salt. Cover tightly.

3 Bake 2 hours or until beef is almost tender. Turn beef over. Scatter apricots and prunes around meat. Mix remaining ingredients and pour over all. Cover and bake 1 hour or until beef is very tender.

4 Lift beef onto a cutting board. Let stand 10 minutes, then cut in thin slices across the grain. Place on serving platter. With a slotted spoon, remove apricots and prunes and arrange around beef. Skim fat from pan juices. Spoon juices over the beef and serve the rest from a gravy boat.

TIME: 3 hr 25 min

SERVES 10

PER SERVING: 486 cal, 35 g pro, 20 g car, 3 g fiber, 29 g fat (11 g saturated fat), 120 mg chol, 333 mg sod

TIP This pot roast, fragrant with Middle Eastern spices, is also delicious served with steamed spinach drizzled with olive oil and lemon juice and with instant couscous prepared with chicken broth instead of water.

INSTANT FRUIT FIXUPS

- Add dried fruit to meat stews.
- Stir diced cantaloupe into curried chicken salad.
- Add coarsely chopped peaches, pears or apples to tomato salsa and serve with grilled or broiled fish.
- Add orange segments to Asian stir-fries.
- Wrap thinly sliced smoked turkey around wedges of mango or honeydew melon.
- Add seedless grapes to a salad of tender greens.

TIME: 2 hr 20 min

SERVES 6

PER SERVING: 370 cal,
  27 g pro, 44 g car, 8 g fiber,
  10 g fat (3 g saturated fat),
  52 mg chol, 1,044 mg sod

TIP *Good over egg noodles.*

TIP *If you refrigerate this stew to serve another night, it will thicken. Add some broth or water to thin.*

Beef Stew with Lentils and Autumn Vegetables

1 lb well-trimmed boneless beef chuck, cut in 1-in. chunks
1/2 tsp salt
1/4 tsp pepper
1 1/2 Tbsp vegetable oil
1 large onion, coarsely chopped (1 1/4 cups)
1 Tbsp minced garlic
3 Tbsp all-purpose flour
5 cups beef broth
2 large Yukon Gold or all-purpose potatoes (1 lb),
   cut in 1-in. chunks (2 1/2 cups)
1 small rutabaga (1 lb), peeled and cut in 1-in. chunks
   (3 cups)
3 medium carrots, cut in 1-in. chunks (1 1/4 cups)
3/4 cup brown lentils, rinsed and picked over
8 oz Swiss chard (1/2 bunch), leaves and stalks thinly sliced
   (4 1/2 cups)

1 Sprinkle beef with salt and pepper. Heat oil in 4- to 5-qt pot over medium heat. Add beef and brown on all sides, 3 to 5 minutes. Add onion and garlic and cook, stirring occasionally, 3 minutes or until lightly browned. Stir in flour and cook 1 minute. Add broth, bring to boil, reduce heat, cover and simmer 1 hour.

2 Add potatoes, rutabaga, carrots and lentils, return to a boil, reduce heat, cover and simmer 25 to 30 minutes until beef, vegetables and lentils are almost tender.

3 Add Swiss chard and simmer, uncovered, 5 to 10 minutes until leaves are wilted and stalks are tender.

3-Bean Beef Chili

1 Tbsp olive oil

3 lb lean beef chuck, cut for stew

2 cups chopped onions

3 cans (14 oz each) diced tomatoes with chiles

2 cups water

1 can (15 oz) tomato sauce

12 oz beer or water

1/3 cup chili powder

3 Tbsp minced garlic

1 Tbsp ground cumin

2 tsp salt

1 tsp dried oregano

1/2 tsp ground cinnamon

1 can each (15 to 16 oz each) black beans, pinto beans and kidney beans, rinsed

1/2 cup chopped fresh cilantro

ACCOMPANIMENTS: sour cream, chopped cilantro and red onion and shredded Monterey Jack or Cheddar cheese

TIME: About 2 hr 30 min

SERVES 12

PER SERVING: 310 cal, 29 g pro, 25 g car, 9 g fiber, 11 g fat (3 g saturated fat), 74 mg chol, 1,340 mg sod

PLANNING TIP *The chili (without cilantro) can be refrigerated up to 4 days or frozen up to 2 weeks. To serve, reheat and add cilantro.*

1 Heat 1 1/2 tsp oil in a 5- to 6-qt pot over medium-high heat. Add half the beef; sauté 5 minutes or until browned. Remove with a slotted spoon to a bowl. Repeat with remaining oil and beef; add to bowl.

2 Add onions to drippings in pot; sauté 5 minutes until golden. Add remaining ingredients except beans and cilantro; bring to a boil. Add beef, partially cover and simmer, stirring occasionally, 2 hours or until beef is very tender.

3 Stir in beans; heat through. Remove from heat and stir in cilantro. Serve with bowls of accompaniments.

SERVES 6

PER SERVING: 594 cal,
  31 g pro, 57 g car, 9 g fiber,
  29 g fat (12 g saturated fat),
  93 mg chol, 1,327 mg sod

TIP *You'll need a skillet that's
    at least 2 in. deep and 10 in.
    across the bottom.*

Chuck Wagon Tortillas

1 lb lean ground beef
1 Tbsp minced garlic
1 1/2 Tbsp chili powder
1 1/2 tsp ground cumin
1 jar (18 oz) baked beans
1 can (14 1/2 oz) stewed tomatoes
1 can (11 oz) vacuum-packed corn
1 can (4 oz) chopped green chiles
1/4 cup bottled barbecue sauce
4 burrito-size flour tortillas
1 1/2 cups shredded pepperjack cheese (6 oz)
*ACCOMPANIMENTS: shredded lettuce, chopped red onion,
    sour cream*

1 Cook beef and garlic in a large nonstick skillet (see Tip) over medium-high heat, breaking up clumps of meat with a spoon, 4 minutes or until no longer pink. Stir in chili powder and cumin. Cook 1 minute longer.

2 Stir in beans, tomatoes, corn, chiles and barbecue sauce. Heat 2 to 3 minutes, then pour into a bowl. Remove skillet from heat, wipe clean with a paper towel, then lightly coat with nonstick cooking spray.

3 Lay 1 tortilla in skillet. Spread evenly with 1 1/2 cups beef mixture, then sprinkle with 1/3 cup cheese. Repeat layers 3 times, ending with remaining 1/2 cup cheese.

4 Cover and cook over low heat 15 minutes, or until cheese melts and stack is hot in center. Cut in wedges; serve with accompaniments.

TIME: 28 min

SERVES 4

PER SERVING: 735 cal,
  46 g pro, 55 g car, 5 g fiber,
  39 g fat (16 g saturated fat),
  121 mg chol, 1,629 mg sod

FYI *A cross between broccoli and Chinese kale, broccolini is sweet with a peppery bite and delicate crunch.*

One at a time, take the noodles from the soaking water, tear them in half lengthwise and add to the skillet.

Lazy Lasagna

8 oven-ready lasagna noodles (from an 8-oz box)
1 lb ground beef round
1 bell pepper, preferably yellow or red, cut in narrow strips
1/2 cup water
1 bunch (about 6 oz) broccolini (see FYI), ends trimmed, or 3 cups broccoli florets
1 jar (26 oz) marinara sauce or arrabbiata (a spicy-hot tomato-based sauce)
1 cup part-skim ricotta cheese
1 cup (4 oz) pizza shreds (a blend of mozzarella, provolone, Parmesan and Romano cheeses) or other shredded cheese blend
GARNISH: shredded basil leaves

1 Soak noodles in hot water to cover 5 to 8 minutes until softened, being careful they don't stick together.

2 Meanwhile heat a 10- or 12-in. skillet over medium-high heat. Add beef and bell pepper and cook, stirring with a wooden spoon to break up clumps of beef, 6 minutes or until meat is no longer pink. Add water and broccolini. Reduce heat, cover and simmer about 3 minutes until broccolini is crisp-tender. Stir in marinara sauce; reduce heat to medium-low.

3 Take noodles from water, tear in half lengthwise (see cooking lesson, *left*) and add to skillet. Stir to mix and coat. Dot with spoonfuls ricotta; sprinkle with cheese shreds.

4 Cover and simmer 5 to 8 minutes until cheese melts. Remove from heat; garnish with basil. Serve from skillet.

Skillet Tamale Pie

12 oz lean ground beef
1 cup chopped scallions
1 jar (14 oz) spaghetti sauce (about 1 3/4 cups)
1 can (15 oz) black beans, rinsed
1 Tbsp chili powder
1 tsp ground cumin
3/4 cup water
1 box (8 1/2 oz) corn muffin mix
1 can (8 1/2 oz) cream-style corn
1 can (4 1/2 oz) chopped green chiles
1/4 cup milk
1 large egg

1 Cook beef and 3/4 cup of the scallions in a large nonstick skillet over medium-high heat 2 to 3 minutes, breaking up beef with a wooden spoon, until no longer pink. Stir in spaghetti sauce, beans, chili powder, cumin and water. Bring to a boil, reduce heat and simmer 10 to 12 minutes to develop flavors and thicken sauce slightly.

2 Meanwhile mix muffin mix, corn, chiles, milk, egg and remaining 1/4 cup scallions (mixture will be soupy).

3 Spoon muffin mixture over beef mixture to cover. Cover skillet and continue simmering 12 to 14 minutes until top looks dry and a pick inserted in topping comes out with slightly moist crumbs.

TIME: 40 min

SERVES 4

PER SERVING: 739 cal, 28 g pro, 86 g car, 7 g fiber, 32 g fat (11 g saturated fat), 119 mg chol, 1,575 mg sod

Smothered Pork Chops

1 tsp each ground ginger and salt
1/2 tsp each ground cinnamon and pepper
4 well-trimmed 1-in.-thick pork loin chops (about 8 oz each)
2 tsp vegetable oil
1 each large onion and red bell pepper, thinly sliced
1 can (8 oz) sliced pineapple in juice
1/2 cup dried apricots, cut in half (see cooking lesson, right)
GARNISH: chopped parsley

1 Mix ginger, salt, cinnamon and pepper on wax paper. Press both sides of chops in seasonings to coat.

2 Heat oil in a nonstick 10- or 12-in. skillet over medium-high heat. Add chops and cook 2 minutes per side or until browned. Remove from skillet; set aside.

3 Add onion and bell pepper to drippings in skillet. Cook, stirring often, 4 minutes to wilt vegetables. Add pineapple and juice, and apricots; place chops on top. Reduce heat, cover and simmer 10 minutes or until pork is cooked through. Sprinkle with parsley.

TIME: 26 min

SERVES 4

PER SERVING: 371 cal,
39 g pro, 26 g car, 3 g fiber,
12 g fat (4 g saturated fat),
102 mg chol, 677 mg sod

TIP *Mashed potatoes go well with this.*

Use kitchen scissors to snip the apricots in half. (To cut sticky dried fruit such as prunes, oil the scissor blades from time to time.)

TIME: 30 min

SERVES 6

PER SERVING: 327 cal,
18 g pro, 51 g car, 2 g fiber,
9 g fat (4 g saturated fat),
50 mg chol, 1,864 mg sod

TIP *Good with green beans.*

Ham, Apples and Rice

2 1/4 cups apple juice
1/2 cup dried cranberries
2 Tbsp butter or margarine
3/4 tsp salt
1/4 tsp pepper, or to taste
2 Golden Delicious apples
4 scallions
1 cup uncooked converted long-grain rice
12-oz chunk baked Virginia ham

1 Bring juice, cranberries, butter, salt and pepper to boil in a 10-in. nonstick skillet.

2 Meanwhile peel apples, cut in quarters, core and dice; slice scallions, separating white from green.

3 Stir rice, apples and white of scallions into boiling liquid in skillet. Return to a boil, reduce heat, cover and simmer 20 minutes or until rice is tender.

4 Meanwhile cut ham in bite-size pieces. When rice is done, stir in ham and green part of scallions. Cover; let stand 5 minutes before serving.

Pork and Apple Stew with Dumplings

1/2 cup 1% lowfat milk
2 Tbsp flour
1 Tbsp plus 1 tsp oil
1 lb pork shoulder (for stew), cut in 3/4-in. pieces
1 small onion, coarsely chopped
2 ribs celery, thinly sliced
2 cups bagged baby carrots
3/4 tsp each dried rosemary and thyme
3/4 tsp salt
4 cups chicken broth (see Note)
2 medium apples, halved, cored and cut in 1/2-in. pieces
1 cup frozen green peas

1 Put milk and flour in a jar with a tight-fitting lid. Shake until blended; set aside.

2 Heat oil in a 4- to 5-qt Dutch oven over medium-high heat. Add pork and sauté 2 minutes until no longer pink. Remove with a slotted spoon to a plate.

3 Add onion, celery and carrots to pot. Cook over medium heat about 5 minutes until onion and celery have softened. Add pork, rosemary, thyme and salt; cook 1 minute until fragrant. Add broth, cover and bring to a boil.

4 Shake jar to remix milk mixture. Stir into stew, bring to a simmer and cook 3 minutes or until slightly thickened and creamy.

5 Meanwhile make Dumplings Dough, *right*.

6 Stir apples and peas into stew and return to a simmer. Drop 12 spoonfuls dough onto stew. Cook 5 minutes, cover and cook 10 minutes more or until a toothpick inserted in center of a dumpling comes out clean. Serve immediately.

TIME: 50 min

SERVES 4

PER SERVING: 587 cal, 30 g pro, 53 g car, 7 g fiber, 28 g fat (9 g saturated fat), 83 mg chol, 1,952 mg sod

NOTE For a slightly sweeter stew, replace 1/2 cup broth with apple cider or juice.

DUMPLINGS DOUGH

3/4 cup plus 1 Tbsp flour
1 1/2 tsp baking powder
1/4 tsp salt
1/4 cup chopped fresh parsley
1/2 cup 1% lowfat milk

Mix flour, baking powder and salt in a medium bowl. Stir in parsley, then milk just until blended.

TIME: 1 hr 50 min

SERVES 6

PER SERVING: 344 cal,
  19 g pro, 35 g car, 5 g fiber,
  15 g fat (8 g saturated fat),
  49 mg chol, 878 mg sod

TIP *Use a food processor to slice the potatoes quickly and evenly.*

Scalloped Potatoes, Ham and Spinach

1 can (10 3/4 oz) 98%-fat-free cream of celery soup
1/2 cup reduced-fat sour cream
1/4 cup shredded onion
*2 boxes (10 oz each) frozen chopped spinach, thawed and
    squeezed dry*
1/8 tsp ground nutmeg
2 1/2 lb baking potatoes, peeled and thinly sliced (see Tip)
1 1/2 cups (6 oz) shredded Cheddar cheese
12 thin slices (about 4 oz) deli-style baked Virginia ham

1 Heat oven to 350°F. Lightly coat a shallow 2-qt baking dish with nonstick spray.

2 Mix soup, sour cream, onion and 1/4 cup water in a large bowl. Mix spinach, nutmeg and 3/4 cup of the soup mixture in a medium bowl. Add potatoes to bowl with remaining soup mixture; toss to coat.

3 Layer half the potatoes over bottom of prepared baking dish. Sprinkle with 1/2 cup cheese, then cover with half the ham, slices overlapping. Top with spinach mixture, then remaining ham, half the remaining cheese and remaining potatoes. Cover tightly with foil.

4 Bake 1 hour 20 minutes or until potatoes are tender when pierced through the foil. Uncover and sprinkle with rest of cheese. Bake uncovered 5 minutes until cheese melts.

Super-Quick Cassoulet

2 tsp olive oil
1/4 cup seasoned dried bread crumbs
1 Tbsp grated Parmesan cheese
1 cup chopped onion
1/2 cup dry white wine or water
1/2 tsp each dried thyme and minced garlic
2 cups bottled chunky-style marinara sauce
2 cups (8 oz) bite-size chunks ham
1 can (19 oz) cannellini beans, rinsed
GARNISH: chopped parsley

1 Heat 1 tsp oil in a large nonstick skillet over medium-high heat. Add bread crumbs and stir 2 minutes or until toasted. Scrape into a small bowl and stir in Parmesan cheese; set aside. Wipe skillet clean.

2 Heat remaining 1 tsp oil in skillet. Add onion; sauté 5 minutes or until golden. Add wine, thyme and garlic; cook 1 minute until most of wine has evaporated.

3 Stir in sauce, ham and beans, bring to a simmer, cover and cook 3 minutes to blend flavors. Spoon into serving bowls; sprinkle with the crumbs and parsley.

TIME: 18 min

SERVES 4

PER SERVING: 373 cal,
    21 g pro, 39 g car, 8 g fiber,
    14 g fat (3 g saturated fat),
    33 mg chol, 1,925 mg sod

SERVES 4

PER SERVING: 460 cal,
  21 g pro, 56 g car, 6 g fiber,
  18 g fat (6 g saturated fat),
  37 mg chol, 1,307 mg sod

Cincinnati Skillet Spaghetti

6 oz chorizo sausage (about 2 links), thinly sliced
1 lb zucchini, halved lengthwise, then sliced in 1/3-in.-wide pieces

SAUCE
  1 can (14 1/2 oz) diced tomatoes with green chiles
  1 can (8 oz) tomato sauce
  1 Tbsp chili powder
  1 tsp ground cumin
  1/4 tsp ground cinnamon
8 oz thin spaghetti
GARNISH: sliced scallions

1 Sauté chorizo in a large nonstick skillet over medium heat 3 minutes or until edges start to brown. Drain on paper towels.

2 Sauté zucchini in same skillet 5 minutes or until lightly browned. Remove to a bowl.

3 Combine Sauce ingredients and 1 1/2 cups water in skillet and bring to a boil. Break spaghetti in thirds, stir into sauce and return to a gentle boil. Cook, uncovered, stirring often, 4 to 5 minutes until pasta is limp.

4 Stir in sausage, reduce heat, cover and simmer 6 to 8 minutes, stirring often, until pasta is firm-tender and most of the liquid is absorbed, but dish is still saucy. Stir in zucchini; sprinkle with scallions.

Italian Pork Roast with Vegetables

1 Tbsp each fennel seeds and chopped garlic
1 1/2 tsp salt
1 tsp each dried rosemary and freshly ground pepper
1 boneless pork loin roast (about 2 lb)

VEGETABLES
   3 bell peppers, quartered and seeded
   1 1/2 lb small red potatoes, halved
   2 medium red onions, cut in 1-in. wedges
   1 1/2 Tbsp olive oil
   1 tsp each salt and crushed dried rosemary (see Tip)

1 Heat oven to 350°F. Lightly coat a 15 1/2 x 10 1/2-in. rimmed baking sheet with nonstick spray.

2 Put fennel seeds, garlic, salt, rosemary and pepper on a cutting board. Chop with a sharp knife until mixture forms a paste. Rub all over pork. Place in the center of the baking sheet.

3 VEGETABLES: Toss all ingredients in a large bowl to mix. Scatter around meat.

4 Roast 50 minutes or until an instant-read thermometer inserted in center of meat registers 155°F to 160°F and vegetables are nearly tender.

5 Remove pork to a cutting board and cover loosely with foil (the meat will continue to cook).

6 Return vegetables to oven. Increase heat to 450°F and roast 15 minutes more or until tender. Cut roast in 1/2-in.-thick slices. Serve with vegetables and pan juices.

TIME: 1 hr 30 min

SERVES 4

PER SERVING: 521 cal, 36 g pro, 43 g car, 6 g fiber, 23 g fat (7 g saturated fat), 93 mg chol, 1,166 mg sod

TIP *To crush dried rosemary, put the amount called for in the palm of one hand and crush with the thumb of the other hand.*

Time: About 20 min

Serves 4

Per serving: 290 cal,
23 g pro, 29 g car, 5 g fiber,
10 g fat (2 g saturated fat),
56 mg chol, 1,019 mg sod

TIP *Lightly coating the pork with cornstarch forms a thin crust that seals in the juices.*

Pork-Vegetable Stir-Fry

12 oz pork tenderloin, cut crosswise in 1/2-in.-thick slices
2 Tbsp cornstarch (see Tip)
1/3 cup each reduced-sodium soy sauce, pineapple or orange juice, and water
1 tsp minced garlic
4 tsp vegetable oil
2 cups fresh precut bagged broccoli florets
1 red bell pepper, cut in bite-size chunks
1 cup precut bagged matchstick-cut carrots
1 can (14 oz) baby corn nuggets, drained
GARNISH: chopped peanuts and sliced scallions

1 Put pork and 1 Tbsp cornstarch in a large plastic zip-top bag. Seal bag; shake until pork is coated.

2 In a small bowl, whisk soy sauce, juice, water, garlic and remaining 1 Tbsp cornstarch until blended.

3 Heat 2 tsp oil in a large nonstick skillet over medium-high heat until hot, but not smoking. Add pork; stir-fry 3 to 4 minutes until lightly browned and cooked through. Remove to serving platter.

4 Heat remaining 2 tsp oil in skillet, add broccoli, pepper and carrots, and stir-fry 5 minutes until crisp-tender. Stir sauce to reblend, add to skillet and bring to a boil. Simmer 30 seconds until thickened.

5 Stir in corn and pork; heat through. Sprinkle with peanuts and scallions.

Enchilada Frittata with Ham

8 large eggs
1 can (8 3/4 oz) corn kernels, drained
1 can or jar (4 or 4 1/4 oz) chopped or diced green chiles, drained
1 Tbsp vegetable oil
4-oz chunk fully cooked ham, diced (1 cup)
3 scallions, sliced, white and green parts separated
2 tsp minced garlic
1 can (10 oz) enchilada sauce
30 baked corn tortilla chips
1 1/2 cups preshredded Monterey Jack cheese

1 Whisk eggs, corn and chiles in a large bowl to blend.

2 Heat oil in a 10- to 11-in. skillet over medium heat. Add ham, white part of scallions and garlic; cook, stirring, 3 to 4 minutes until scallions are soft.

3 Add egg mixture; stir to mix. Reduce heat to medium-low. Cover skillet; cook 10 minutes or until eggs set on top.

4 Top with enchilada sauce, tortilla chips, cheese and green part of scallions.

5 Cover and cook about 1 minute to melt cheese. Cut in wedges to serve (see Tip).

TIME: 25 min

SERVES 4

PER SERVING: 504 cal,
33 g pro, 27 g car, 2 g fiber,
30 g fat (12 g saturated fat),
487 mg chol, 1,728 mg sod

TIP *Serve with sour cream.*

TIME: 2 hr

SERVES 4

PER SERVING: 347 cal,
  23 g pro, 33 g car, 7 g fiber,
  14 g fat (4 g saturated fat),
  57 mg chol, 1,302 mg sod

NOTE *Ancho chiles are not-too-hot, reddish-brown dried chiles. They begin life as fresh dark-green poblano chiles, the kind usually stuffed to make Chiles Rellenos. Look for ancho chiles in the produce section of your supermarket, or call Dean & DeLuca at 800-221-7714 to order or get their mail-order catalog.*

FYI *Hominy is dried corn kernels from which the hull and germ have been removed. It's available canned, ready-to-eat or dried (which has to be reconstituted). When dried hominy is ground, it's called hominy grits (or just "grits") and is usually cooked with milk or water for breakfast or as a side dish.*

Tex-Mex Pork Stew

1 Tbsp vegetable oil

3/4 lb well-trimmed boneless pork shoulder (Boston butt), cut in 3/4-in. chunks

2 large onions, coarsely chopped (3 cups)

2 Tbsp minced garlic

4 cups chicken broth

2 ancho chiles (see Note), stems and seeds removed, chiles rinsed

1 tsp dried oregano

1 can (15 to 16 oz) white hominy (see FYI) or corn kernels, drained

TOPPINGS: chopped lettuce, tomato and cilantro, sliced radishes, lime wedges and shredded Monterey Jack cheese

1 Heat oil in 3-qt saucepan over medium-high heat. Add pork and brown on all sides, 3 to 5 minutes. Add onions and garlic and cook about 5 minutes, stirring occasionally, until lightly browned.

2 TO COOK ON RANGETOP: Add broth, chiles and oregano. Bring to boil, reduce heat, cover and simmer 1 hour or until pork is tender. Add hominy and simmer, uncovered, 10 minutes. TO COOK IN SLOW-COOKER: Place cooked pork, onions and garlic in cooker along with remaining ingredients except toppings. Cover and cook on high 4 to 5 hours or on low 8 to 10 hours.

3 Using a slotted spoon, skim off and discard any floating chile skin. Pour stew into individual soup bowls, removing any remaining visible chile skin. Serve with bowls of toppings.

Middle Eastern Lamb Stew

1 lemon

1 Tbsp vegetable oil

1 1/2 lb well-trimmed boneless lamb shoulder, cut in
   1 1/2-in. chunks

1 large onion, coarsely chopped (1 1/4 cups)

2 cups chicken broth

1 tsp ground ginger

1 cinnamon stick (about 3 in. long)

1/4 tsp pepper

1/3 cup bite-size pitted prunes, or regular-size pitted prunes,
   cut in half

2 Tbsp honey

GARNISH: toasted blanched slivered almonds

1 Heat oven to 325°F. Have ready a 2- to 3-qt Dutch oven.

2 Using a vegetable peeler, peel yellow part of peel
(zest) from lemon in strips (white part is bitter). Stack
strips, then cut in narrow pieces. Cut lemon in half and
squeeze out juice (you'll need 2 Tbsp). Reserve peel and
juice separately.

3 Heat oil in Dutch oven. Add lamb and brown on all
sides. Add onion and sauté until lightly browned. Add
lemon peel, broth, ginger, cinnamon stick and pepper. Bring
to a boil, cover and place in oven.

4 Bake 1 1/4 hours. Add prunes and lemon juice, cover
and bake 15 minutes longer or until lamb is tender.

5 Using a slotted spoon, remove lamb, prunes and peel
to a serving platter. Place pot over medium heat and stir
honey into sauce. Bring to a boil and cook 3 minutes until
sauce is slightly thickened and syrupy. Pour over lamb;
sprinkle with almonds.

TIME: 2 hr 20 min

SERVES 4

PER SERVING: 378 cal,
   35 g pro, 23 g car, 2 g fiber,
   16 g fat (5 g saturated fat), 112
   mg chol, 622 mg sod

TIP *You can serve with couscous and sautéed sliced zucchini and/or yellow squash
flavored with minced garlic.*

TIME: 2 hr 10 min

SERVES 6

PER SERVING: 474 cal,
  44 g pro, 38 g car, 9 g fiber,
  16 g fat (5 g saturated fat),
  114 mg chol, 471 mg sod

Braised Lamb and White Beans

*Six 1-in.-thick shoulder lamb chops (about 10 oz each),
  fat trimmed*
1/4 cup flour
1 1/2 Tbsp olive oil
1 1/2 cups finely chopped onions
1 Tbsp minced garlic
1 cup chicken broth
1/2 tsp each dried rosemary and thyme
2 tsp freshly grated lemon peel
*2 lb butternut squash, halved, peeled, seeded and cut in
  1 1/4-in. chunks*
2 cans (15 oz each) cannellini beans, rinsed
GARNISH: chopped parsley

1 Heat oven to 325°F. Have ready a 4- to 5-qt stovetop-to-oven casserole with a tight-fitting lid.

2 Coat chops with flour. Heat oil in casserole. Add chops and cook until browned on both sides. Remove to a plate.

3 Add onions and garlic to casserole. Sauté until onions are translucent. Add broth and herbs. Bring to a gentle boil, scraping up browned bits on bottom of casserole. Stir in lemon peel. Add chops and cover with lid or with foil, then lid.

4 Bake 1 hour, then stir in squash. Cover and bake 30 minutes. Gently stir in beans, cover and bake 15 minutes or until meat and squash are fork-tender.

5 Remove chops, vegetables and beans to serving platter with a slotted spoon. Cover loosely with foil. Skim off and discard fat from liquid in casserole. Boil gently until slightly thickened and reduced to about 2 cups. Serve with chops; sprinkle with parsley.

Veal Milanese Insalata

2 large eggs
2/3 cup plain dry bread crumbs
1/4 cup grated Parmesan cheese
Four 4-oz veal cutlets for scallopini
3 Tbsp olive oil
3 oz mesclun (4 packed cups)
1/2 a medium bulb fennel, thinly sliced lengthwise
12 grape tomatoes, cut in half
1/4 cup thinly sliced red onion
1/4 cup bottled balsamic vinaigrette
GARNISH: shaved Parmesan (see Tip)

1 Beat eggs in a rimmed plate. Mix crumbs and grated cheese in another plate. Coat 1 cutlet at a time with egg then crumb mixture.

2 Heat 1 1/2 Tbsp oil in a large nonstick skillet over medium heat. Add 2 cutlets; cook 1 to 1 1/2 minutes per side until golden and just cooked through. Repeat with remaining oil and cutlets.

3 Meanwhile put next 4 ingredients in a large bowl.

4 Just before serving, add vinaigrette to salad; toss to coat. Serve on cutlets; sprinkle with Parmesan.

TIME: 21 min

SERVES 4

PER SERVING: 425 cal, 32 g pro, 21 g car, 3 g fiber, 23 g fat (5 g saturated fat), 199 mg chol, 555 mg sod

TIP To get shavings, pull a vegetable peeler across a chunk of room-temperature Parmesan cheese.

TIME: 30 min

SERVES 4

PER SERVING: 468 cal,
29 g pro, 70 g car, 5 g fiber,
7 g fat (4 g saturated fat),
140 mg chol, 934 mg sod

TIP Make sure the label on the can says coconut milk, not cream of coconut or coconut water.

NOTE Serve with a green salad and pass a bottle of hot-pepper sauce at the table.

Brazilian Coconut Shrimp and Rice

1 can (14 oz) light coconut milk (see Tip)
2 medium onions, halved lengthwise, thinly sliced crosswise
1 Tbsp minced garlic
1 box (8 oz) yellow rice mix
2 cups frozen green peas
2/3 cup water
1 lb raw medium shrimp, peeled and deveined
1/4 cup chopped fresh cilantro
3 Tbsp fresh lime juice
GARNISH: lime wedges

1 Heat coconut milk in a large nonstick skillet over medium-high heat. Add onions and garlic, reduce heat, cover and simmer 3 minutes or until onions are crisp-tender.

2 Stir in rice mix, frozen peas and water. Cover and simmer 15 minutes or until almost all liquid is absorbed and the rice is firm-tender.

3 Stir in shrimp, cover and simmer 5 to 6 minutes, stirring once or twice, until shrimp are opaque in center. Stir in cilantro and lime juice. Garnish with lime wedges.

Tunisian Tuna on Couscous

2 cups water
1 box (10 oz) plain couscous
1 tsp salt
1 Tbsp oil, preferably olive
2 medium zucchini, cut in 3/4-in. chunks
1 medium onion, cut in narrow strips
1 can (19 oz) chickpeas, rinsed
1 can (16 oz) tomato sauce
1 tsp ground cumin
1/8 tsp ground cinnamon
1 can (6 oz) solid white tuna in oil, drained
8 large pimiento-stuffed green olives, sliced

1 Bring water to boil in a large nonstick skillet. Mix couscous and 1/2 tsp salt in a serving bowl, stir in the water, cover and let stand.

2 Heat oil in skillet over medium heat. Add zucchini and onions and sauté 3 to 4 minutes until both are crisp-tender.

3 Stir in chickpeas, tomato sauce, cumin, remaining 1/2 tsp salt and the cinnamon. Simmer uncovered 5 minutes to develop flavors. Remove from heat.

4 Add tuna, breaking up large chunks; stir in olives. Uncover couscous and fluff with a fork; serve topped with the Tunisian Tuna.

TIME: 18 min

SERVES 4

PER SERVING: 522 cal, 28 g pro, 81 g car, 9 g fiber, 11 g fat (1 g saturated fat), 13 mg chol, 1,778 mg sod

FYI *The couscous requires no cooking, only a short soak in boiling water.*

TIME: 25 min

SERVES 4

PER SERVING: 442 cal,
22 g pro, 72 g car, 3 g fiber,
8 g fat (4 g saturated fat),
107 mg chol, 742 mg sod

TIP *Make sure the label on
the can says coconut milk,
not cream of coconut or
coconut water.*

Thai Shrimp and Rice

1 tsp vegetable oil
1/2 cup sliced scallions
1 Tbsp chopped garlic
1 can (14 oz) light coconut milk (see Tip)
1 1/2 cups jasmine rice or converted white rice
1 cup shredded carrots (from a 10-oz bag shredded carrots)
1 tsp salt
12 oz raw medium shrimp, peeled and deveined
8 oz fresh snow peas
2 tsp freshly grated lime peel
GARNISH: lime wedges and chopped cilantro

1 Heat oil in a large nonstick skillet over medium heat. Add scallions and garlic; sauté 1 to 2 minutes until aromatic.

2 Pour coconut milk into a 4-cup liquid measure and add enough water to make 3 1/4 cups. Add to skillet and bring to a boil. Add rice, carrots and salt. Cover, reduce heat and simmer 12 minutes or until rice is nearly tender.

3 Stir in shrimp, snow peas, lime peel and, if rice looks dry, another 1/4 cup water. Bring to a simmer, cover and cook 3 to 4 minutes until shrimp are cooked through and the snow peas are crisp-tender. Garnish with lime wedges and chopped cilantro.

Quick French Fish and Potato Stew

2 large cloves garlic, peeled
2 tsp fennel seeds
1/2 tsp each dried thyme and salt
2 tsp olive oil, preferably extra-virgin
1 1/2 cups each chopped onions and thinly sliced carrots
4 cups chicken broth
2 lb (about 4 medium) baking potatoes, peeled and cut in 1-in. chunks
1 can (14 oz) diced tomatoes
1 1/2 lb cod or scrod fillets, cut in 1-in. chunks
1/2 to 1 tsp freshly ground pepper

1 Put garlic, fennel seeds, thyme and salt on a cutting board. Chop, then mash to a paste with the side of a large, heavy knife.

2 Heat oil in a 4- to 5-qt pot over medium heat. Add garlic mixture and cook, stirring, 1 minute or until fragrant. Stir in onions and carrots. Cook, stirring often, 5 minutes or until onions are translucent.

3 Stir in chicken broth and potatoes. Bring to a boil, reduce heat, cover and simmer 15 to 20 minutes until potatoes are tender. Stir in tomatoes, increase heat to medium and gently boil 2 to 3 minutes.

4 Stir in fish. Cover and simmer 5 minutes or until fish is opaque at center. Stir in pepper. Ladle into serving bowl.

TIME: 50 min

SERVES 6

PER SERVING: 265 cal,
26 g pro, 32 g car, 4 g fiber,
4 g fat (1 g saturated fat),
49 mg chol, 1,050 mg sod

TIP *Serve with French bread to sop up the juices.*

TIME: 27 min

SERVES 4

PER SERVING: 189 cal,
  29 g pro, 7 g car, 0 g fiber,
  6 g fat (2 g saturated fat),
  55 mg chol, 266 mg sod

TIPS If herbs and black pepper
  aren't your thing, use the
  smaller amount.

When testing the fish for doneness, open the packets carefully
to avoid the hot steam that
will escape.

NOTE Fragrant with fresh
  herbs, this delicious swordfish
  is best accompanied by
  a rice dish and a green
  salad. The packets can be
  prepared in the morning or
  the day before and kept in
  the refrigerator.

Peppered Lemon Swordfish Steaks

1 1/4-lb swordfish steak (1 in. thick), cut in 4 equal pieces
2 lemons, thinly sliced, seeds removed
1/2 red onion, thinly sliced
1 to 2 Tbsp minced fresh rosemary or 1 to 2 tsp dried,
  crumbled (see Tip)
1/2 to 1 Tbsp minced fresh thyme leaves, or 1/2 to 1 tsp dried
1/2 to 1 tsp coarsely ground black pepper
1/4 tsp salt

1 Heat oven to 500°F or heat charcoal or gas grill.

2 Place each piece of fish on center of a double-layer
piece of foil (or 1 layer heavy-duty foil). Top evenly with
remaining ingredients.

3 Make packets by bringing up 2 sides of foil to meet
in center, folding edges over, then folding edges of each
end together. Allowing room for packets to expand, crimp
the edges. If baking, place packets on a baking sheet.

4 Bake or grill 10 to 12 minutes until fish is opaque in
center (see Tip).

Shrimp and Corn Chowder

4 slices bacon, stacked and diced
1 each medium onion and red bell pepper, diced
3 Tbsp all-purpose flour
1 lb red-skinned potatoes, cut in 1/2-in. chunks (3 cups)
2 cups whole milk
1 can (14 1/2 oz) chicken broth
1 can (14 1/2 oz) whole-kernel corn, drained
1 Tbsp fresh thyme leaves or 1 tsp dried
3/4 tsp salt
1/2 tsp black pepper
1 lb raw medium shrimp, peeled, deveined and cut bite-size

1 Heat a 3- to 4-qt saucepan over medium heat. Add bacon; cook until crisp. Remove with a slotted spoon, drain well on paper towels and reserve.

2 Drain off all but 1 Tbsp fat. Add onion and bell pepper and cook, stirring as needed, 5 minutes or until soft. Add flour; stir until blended with fat. Stir in remaining ingredients except shrimp.

3 Bring to a boil, stirring to bottom of saucepan and taking care to get into corners. Reduce heat, partially cover and simmer 10 minutes, stirring occasionally, or until potatoes are tender. Add the shrimp and simmer a minute or 2 until cooked through. Ladle into soup plates and sprinkle with bacon. Serve immediately.

TIME: 50 min

SERVES 4

PER SERVING: 436 cal,
   31 g pro, 50 g car, 5 g fiber,
   13 g fat (5 g saturated fat),
   164 mg chol, 1,337 mg sod

SERVES 4

PER SERVING: 573 cal,
44 g pro, 42 g car, 4 g fiber,
26 g fat (8 g saturated fat),
100 mg chol, 634 mg sod

TIP Make sure the label on
the can says coconut milk,
not cream of coconut or
coconut water.

TIP Hold each asparagus
lengthwise in both hands,
one hand close to the bottom end. Bend the aspara-
gus until it breaks naturally.
Discard the thick bottom
end.

Salmon and Vegetables with Coconut Sauce

1 can (14 oz) light coconut milk (see Tip)
4 scallions, sliced, white part separated from green
2 tsp each minced garlic and fresh ginger
1/4 tsp each salt and pepper
1 1/2-lb piece salmon fillet, preferably center-cut, skin removed,
   cut in 4 pieces
1 lb asparagus, woody ends snapped off (see Tip),
   spears cut in thirds
1 cup preshredded carrots (from a bag)
Eight 1/2-in.-thick slices Italian bread, toasted
ACCOMPANIMENT: lime wedges

1 Put coconut milk, white part of scallion, garlic, ginger, salt and pepper in a large nonstick skillet; stir until well blended. Top with salmon in a single layer; scatter asparagus and carrots over and around the salmon.

2 Bring to a gentle simmer; cover and cook 8 minutes or until salmon is cooked through and asparagus is crisp-tender.

3 Using a broad spatula, transfer salmon to a serving platter. Spoon sauce and vegetables over salmon, then sprinkle with green part of scallions. Serve immediately with the bread and lime wedges to squeeze on the fish.

Salmon-Potato Skillet

1 can (14 1/2 oz) lemon-and-herb-flavored chicken broth
1/2 cup water
1 lb red-skinned potatoes
1 red bell pepper
4 center-cut salmon fillets (5 to 6 oz each)
1/3 cup each thinly sliced white and green part of scallions,
 kept separate
2 Tbsp creamy mustard spread (such as Dijonnaise)

1 Bring broth and water to a boil in a large, deep non-stick skillet (with a lid).

2 Meanwhile scrub and thinly slice potatoes. Add to broth, return to a gentle boil and cook 10 minutes.

3 While potatoes cook, halve, core and thinly slice red pepper. Place salmon on potatoes; top with pepper strips and white part of scallion. Bring to a simmer, cover and cook 10 minutes or until salmon is cooked through and potatoes are tender. Remove skillet from heat.

4 Using a slotted spoon, transfer salmon, vegetables and potatoes to dinner plates. Add mustard and green part of scallion to liquid in skillet; stir until blended. Spoon over the salmon.

TIME: 25 min

SERVES 4

PER SERVING: 407 cal,
 34 g pro, 25 g car, 3 g fiber,
 19 g fat (3 g saturated fat),
 92 mg chol, 584 mg sod

TIME: 45 min

SERVES 4

PER SERVING: 411 cal,
38 g pro, 25 g car, 2 g fiber,
18 g fat (3 g saturated fat),
90 mg chol, 536 mg sod

FYI *In Sicily fresh sardines are stuffed with a filling similar to the one used here.*

TIP *To toast nuts, spread on baking sheet and place in oven as it's heating for 6 to 8 minutes, stirring twice, until toasted.*

NOTE *Farm-raised trout are available in supermarket seafood departments. Ask to have the backbones removed to make stuffing and eating easier.*

Sicilian Stuffed Trout

STUFFING

2/3 cup plain dry bread crumbs

1/3 cup golden raisins, chopped

1/4 cup toasted pine nuts (pignoli) or slivered
  almonds (see Tip)

2 Tbsp each *minced Italian parsley and grated
  Parmesan cheese*

1 Tbsp each *olive oil and fresh lemon juice*

2 tsp *minced garlic*

1/2 tsp *salt*

4 whole rainbow or salmon trout (about 8 oz each),
  backbones removed (see Note)

1 Tbsp olive oil

GARNISH: *lemon slices and parsley sprigs*

1 Heat oven to 375°F. Lightly coat a 15 1/2 x 10 1/2-in. rimmed baking sheet with nonstick spray.

2 Toss Stuffing ingredients with a fork in a medium bowl until well blended.

3 Arrange trout on their sides in one layer in prepared pan. Spoon 1/2 cup stuffing in each cavity. Gently press down on trout to enclose stuffing. With fingertips spread oil on trout to coat. Cover pan tightly with foil.

4 Bake 15 minutes, remove foil and bake 10 minutes more or until an instant-read thermometer inserted in center of stuffing registers at least 160°F and fish is opaque when pierced with a fork at thickest part.

5 Remove with a wide spatula to a serving platter. Garnish with lemon and parsley.

Quick Paella

1 tsp olive oil
1 cup chopped onion
3 oz chorizo sausage, diced
1 can (14 1/2 oz) roasted-garlic-seasoned chicken broth
1 can diced tomatoes in juice, undrained
1 tsp ground turmeric (see FYI)
1/2 tsp salt
1/4 tsp crushed red pepper
1 cup uncooked parboiled (converted) white rice
2 cups frozen petite peas
8 oz medium shrimp, peeled and deveined, tails left on
1/2 cup pimiento-stuffed olives, halved

1 Heat oil in large nonstick skillet. Add onion and chorizo; sauté 5 minutes or until onion is translucent. Stir in broth, tomatoes and their juice, the turmeric, salt and crushed pepper.

2 Bring to a boil, stir in rice, reduce heat to a gentle simmer, cover and cook 15 minutes. Stir in remaining ingredients, return to a simmer, cover and cook 5 minutes or until rice is tender and shrimp are cooked through.

TIME: 45 min

SERVES 4

PER SERVING: 461 cal, 24 g pro, 61 g car, 9 g fiber, 13 g fat (4 g saturated fat), 91 mg chol, 1,732 mg sod

FYI *Paella, a Spanish dish, traditionally gets its slightly pungent flavor and orange-yellow color from expensive saffron. Turmeric does the job for considerably less.*

TIME: About 1 hr 15 min

SERVES 4

Per serving: 280 cal,
23 g pro, 23 g car, 3 g fiber,
13 g fat (3 g saturated fat),
176 mg chol, 1,059 mg sod

NOTE *Cut avocado in half lengthwise around seed; rotate halves to separate. Slide a spoon under seed; remove. Place cut sides down; remove skin with fingers, then cut as directed.*

FYI *The acid in the lime juice will keep the cut-up avocado from darkening.*

Gazpacho with Shrimp, Avocado and Lime

SOUP

1 jar (12 oz) roasted red peppers, drained
1 cucumber, peeled, halved lengthwise; seeds scraped out
2 cups tomato juice
12 oz peeled, deveined cooked medium shrimp
2 plum (Roma) tomatoes
1 avocado
1 small green bell pepper
1/2 small red onion
Fresh chives or parsley (enough for 3 Tbsp minced)
2 Tbsp fresh lime juice
1/2 tsp salt
1/4 tsp pepper
8 Tbsp reduced-fat sour cream

1 SOUP: Put roasted peppers, cucumber and tomato juice in a blender. Blend at medium speed 1 minute or until smooth. Pour into a metal bowl and chill, stirring occasionally, about 1 hour until cold.

2 Meanwhile reserve 4 shrimp for garnish; cut rest in 1/2-in. pieces. Cut tomatoes and avocado (see Note) in 1/2-in. pieces, finely dice bell pepper and onion, and mince chives. Place in a large bowl. Add lime juice, salt and pepper; stir gently with a rubber spatula to mix and coat (see FYI).

3 Mound 1/2 cup shrimp mixture in center of each of 4 soup plates. Pour 1 cup soup around each mound; pat mounds down slightly. Top each with 2 Tbsp sour cream, then remaining shrimp mixture. Garnish with whole shrimp.

Shrimp and Peppers with Parmesan Grits

1 1/2 cups each 1% lowfat milk and water
2 Tbsp minced garlic
3/4 cup instant grits
1 cup grated Parmesan cheese
1 Tbsp vegetable oil
1 each small to medium green, red and yellow bell pepper,
   cut in thin strips
1 medium onion, cut in thin wedges
1 lb large shrimp, peeled and deveined
2 tsp Caribbean jerk seasoning, or to taste

1 Bring milk, water and garlic to a boil in a large non-stick skillet over medium heat. Slowly whisk in grits. Reduce heat, cover and simmer gently, stirring occasionally and scraping bottom of skillet, 8 to 10 minutes until thickened. Remove from heat; stir in cheese. Pour into a serving bowl; cover to keep warm.

2 Clean skillet, add oil and heat over medium heat. Add peppers and onion; cook, stirring occasionally, 6 minutes or until crisp-tender and lightly browned. Stir in shrimp and seasoning; cook, stirring a few times, 3 minutes or until shrimp are cooked through. Serve with the grits.

TIME: 40 min

SERVES 4

PER SERVING: 359 cal,
   32 g pro, 27 g car, 2 g fiber,
   13 g fat (5 g saturated fat),
   159 mg chol, 877 mg sod

Pad Thai

8 oz 1/8-in.-wide flat rice sticks
1/4 cup each bottled fish sauce and seasoned rice vinegar
2 Tbsp fresh lime juice
1 Tbsp sugar
3 Tbsp peanut oil
1 lb raw peeled, deveined shrimp (any size)
1 Tbsp minced garlic
2 large eggs
8 thinly sliced radishes
4 scallions, cut in 1-in. lengths
1/4 cup dry-roasted unsalted peanuts, finely chopped
1/4 cup packed cilantro leaves, finely chopped

1 Soak rice sticks in warm water to cover 20 minutes until softened (see Note).

2 Meanwhile mix fish sauce, seasoned rice vinegar, lime juice and sugar in a cup.

3 Heat 1 Tbsp oil in a large nonstick skillet over medium-high heat. Add shrimp and garlic; sauté 1 to 3 minutes until cooked through. Transfer to a plate.

4 Heat remaining 2 Tbsp oil over medium-high heat. Add eggs; stir just until set. Add radishes, scallions, drained rice sticks and fish-sauce mixture. Cook, stirring, 1 minute or until rice sticks soften and wilt.

5 Place on a serving platter; top with shrimp, peanuts and cilantro. Toss to mix.

TIME: 30 min

SERVES 4

PER SERVING: 568 cal, 31 g pro, 63 g car, 1 g fiber, 21 g fat (4 g saturated fat), 279 mg chol, 1,198 mg sod

FYI *This noodle dish is a favorite in Thailand.*

NOTE *The rice sticks will still be a bit stiff after soaking but will soften while cooking.*

PER SERVING: 427 cal,
25 g pro, 62 g car, 3 g fiber,
8 g fat (5 g saturated fat),
130 mg chol, 740 mg sod

TIP *If your market carries feta cheese with basil and tomatoes, you can use that instead of plain feta, but reduce the basil in the rice cooking water to 1 tsp.*

SKILLET SKILL

- *To keep a nonstick skillet in good condition, use wooden or plastic tools (no matter what the manufacturer says) and avoid the dishwasher.*

- *When a cover is called for, make sure to use a tight-fitting lid. If your skillet is lidless, use a baking sheet or pizza pan.*

Shrimp-Rice Pilaf with Feta Cheese

3 cups water
2 tsp dried basil, crumbled
2 cups frozen broccoli florets (from a 20-oz bag)
1 1/2 cups uncooked converted rice
3/4 lb medium shrimp (about 24)
1/2 tsp salt
4 oz crumbled feta cheese (1/2 cup)

1 Bring water and basil to a boil in a 12-in. skillet.

2 Meanwhile rinse frozen broccoli florets in a colander under running warm water to thaw slightly.

3 Add rice to skillet, return water to a boil, reduce heat to low, cover and cook 13 minutes.

4 While rice cooks, peel and devein shrimp. When rice has cooked 13 minutes, add shrimp, broccoli and salt to skillet and stir to mix well.

5 Cover and cook 7 to 8 minutes longer or until shrimp are opaque in center.

6 Add feta cheese and stir gently until partially melted and rice is lightly coated. Serve immediately.

Spring Vegetable Frittata

3 medium carrots, shredded (1 1/2 cups)
1 lb asparagus, woody ends snapped off (see Tip)
1 Tbsp oil, preferably olive
6 cups frozen country-style hash brown potatoes
  (from a 30-oz bag)
1 tsp salt
8 large eggs, beaten with a fork
6 oz smoked Gouda or mozzarella cheese, shredded (1 1/2 cups)
1/2 cup sliced scallions

1 Bring 1 cup water to a boil in a large nonstick skillet. Add carrots and asparagus, reduce heat, cover and simmer 5 to 6 minutes until asparagus are crisp-tender. Drain well; wipe out skillet.

2 Heat oil in skillet over medium heat. Add potatoes, sprinkle with 1/2 tsp salt and cook 5 minutes until bottoms are lightly browned. Turn with a spatula and press down, pushing some potatoes up the sides of the skillet.

3 Mix remaining 1/2 tsp salt with the eggs; pour mixture over potatoes. Top with the carrots and asparagus. Cover and cook over medium-low heat 10 minutes or until eggs are almost set.

4 Sprinkle with cheese and scallions, cover and cook 2 to 3 minutes to melt cheese.

TIME: 32 min

SERVES 6

PER SERVING: 311 cal,
  19 g pro, 20 g car, 3 g fiber,
  17 g fat (7 g saturated fat),
  323 mg chol, 827 mg sod

TIP Hold each asparagus lengthwise in both hands, one hand close to the bottom end. Bend the asparagus until it breaks naturally. Discard the thick bottom end.

SERVES 4

PER SERVING: 433 cal,
20 g pro, 75 g car, 9 g fiber,
8 g fat (1 g saturated fat),
0 mg chol, 1,429 mg sod

TIP *The perfect accompaniment? Coleslaw.*

Two-Bean Sloppy Joes

*1 can each (15 to 16 oz) black-eyed peas and red kidney
  beans, rinsed*
1 1/2 cups bottled marinara sauce
1 can (14 1/2 oz) no-salt-added diced tomatoes in juice, drained
*1/2 cup each frozen cut green beans and chopped
  green bell pepper*
1 Tbsp Worcestershire sauce
2 tsp red-wine vinegar
1 1/2 tsp chili powder
4 split seeded kaiser or hamburger rolls, toasted

1 Bring all ingredients except rolls to boil in 10- or 12-in. nonstick skillet over medium-high heat. Reduce heat, partially cover and simmer, stirring occasionally, 10 to 15 minutes until peppers are tender.

2 Spoon onto roll bottoms; replace tops.

Tomato and Cheese Strata

10 slices white sandwich bread
4 tomatoes, cut in 1/2-in.-thick slices
4 oz Cheddar cheese, shredded (1 cup)
4 scallions, sliced
2 cups milk
4 large eggs
1/2 tsp salt

1 Lightly grease an 8-in. square baking dish. Place 4 slices of bread over the bottom. Arrange half the tomatoes, half the cheese and half the scallions on the bread. Top with 6 slices bread (overlapping) and remaining tomatoes, cheese and scallions.

2 Whisk milk, eggs and salt until blended. Pour over bread and bake, or cover and refrigerate up to 24 hours.

3 Bake in 350°F oven 40 to 45 minutes until puffed and golden, and knife inserted near center comes out clean.

TIME: 1 hr

SERVES 4

PER SERVING: 470 cal, 24 g pro, 44 g car, 3 g fiber, 22 g fat (11 g saturated fat), 260 mg chol, 938 mg sod

TIME: 25 min

SERVES 4

PER SERVING: 506 cal,
  15 g pro, 55 g car, 6 g fiber,
  27 g fat (6 g saturated fat),
  17 mg chol, 834 mg sod

Hold each asparagus lengthwise in both hands, one hand close to the bottom end. Bend the asparagus until it breaks naturally. Discard the thick bottom end.

Look for tubs of pesto in your market's fresh pasta or dairy section.

Gnocchi Primavera

1 bunch (about 1 lb) asparagus, woody ends snapped off, spears cut crosswise in thirds (see Tip)
2 medium yellow summer squash, cut in half lengthwise, then crosswise in 1/2-in. pieces
1 bag (16 oz) frozen gnocchi
3/4 cup basil pesto (see Note)
1/2 cup reduced-fat sour cream
1 pt (12 oz) grape tomatoes, cut in half
GARNISH: grated Parmesan cheese (optional)

1 Bring a large pot of lightly salted water to a boil. Have ready a shallow serving bowl.

2 Add asparagus and squash to pot; return to a boil and boil 1 minute. Add gnocchi; cover pot just until water returns to a boil. Uncover and cook 2 minutes more or until gnocchi float to surface and vegetables are crisp-tender. Drain in a colander; transfer to serving bowl.

3 Mix pesto and sour cream in pot. Stir in tomatoes. Pour over gnocchi; toss gently to mix and coat. Serve with Parmesan cheese, if desired.

Hearty Pumpkin Chowder

2 Tbsp stick butter
1 cup each *diced onion and celery*
4 cups *3/4- to 1-in. chunks peeled pumpkin or butternut squash*
   (see The Right Pumpkin, right)
2 Tbsp each *minced, peeled fresh ginger and garlic*
3 cups chicken broth
8 oz red-skinned potatoes, scrubbed and cut in 3/4-in. chunks
1 1/2 cups frozen lima beans
1 cup frozen or fresh corn kernels
1 small red bell pepper, seeded and diced
8-oz chunk ham, cut in bite-size pieces
4 cups 1% lowfat milk
1/3 cup flour
3/4 tsp salt
1/2 tsp nutmeg, preferably freshly grated

1 Melt butter in a 4-qt or larger saucepan over medium heat. Add onion, celery, pumpkin, ginger and garlic; sauté 5 to 6 minutes until onions and celery are tender.

2 Stir in broth, potatoes, lima beans, corn and bell pepper. Bring to a boil, reduce heat, cover and simmer 15 minutes or until vegetables are tender. Add ham.

3 Meanwhile whisk milk, flour, salt and nutmeg in a medium bowl until well blended.

4 Stir into saucepan, bring to a gentle boil and, stirring occasionally, cook 3 minutes or until chowder has thickened slightly.

TIME: 1 hr

SERVES 6

PER SERVING: 339 cal,
   20 g pro, 43 g car, 5 g fiber,
   11 g fat (5 g saturated fat),
   38 mg chol, 1,455 mg sod

THE RIGHT PUMPKIN

Eating pumpkins, usually referred to as pie or sugar pumpkins, tend to be smaller and have finer-grained flesh and a sweeter, more delicate flavor than field pumpkins, which are the kind used for jack-o'-lanterns.

If your market doesn't carry eating pumpkins, you can substitute butternut squash, which has a similar color, texture and yield.

Yields vary depending on the thickness of the skin, how you peel it (paring knife versus vegetable peeler) and the size of the seed cavity. On average, a peeled 2-lb pumpkin or butternut squash will give you about 6 cups of 3/4- to 1-in. chunks.

TIME: 1 hr 15 min

SERVES 6

PER SERVING: 336 cal,
  13 g pro, 24 g car, 0 g fiber,
  20 g fat (10 g saturated fat),
  177 mg chol, 547 mg sod

TIP *For a crisper crust, prebake the pie shell as directed on box.*

Spring Vegetable Quiche

1 refrigerated ready-to-use pie crust
2 cups whole milk
1 box (0.9 oz) spring vegetable soup, dip and recipe mix
4 large eggs
4 oz Swiss cheese, shredded (1 cup)

1 Following directions on box, line a 9-in. pie plate with pie crust (see Tip).

2 Pour milk into a 4-cup measure, add soup mix and let soak at least 10 minutes.

3 Meanwhile heat oven to 350°F.

4 Beat eggs in a medium bowl with a fork until blended. Stir in milk mixture.

5 Sprinkle 3/4 cup cheese over crust. Add egg mixture; sprinkle rest of cheese on top.

6 Bake 45 minutes or until tip of a knife inserted in center comes out clean. Let stand 10 minutes before cutting in wedges.

Middle Eastern Chickpeas
with Couscous

1 Tbsp olive oil
1 each medium yellow squash and zucchini, cut in half
  lengthwise, then crosswise in 1/2-in.-thick slices
2 cans (14 1/2 oz each) diced tomatoes with onion and garlic
1 can (19 oz) chickpeas, rinsed
20 pitted kalamata olives (see Tip)
1/3 cup raisins
1 tsp ground cumin
1 tsp ground coriander (optional)
1/2 tsp freshly ground pepper
1 box (5.6 oz) couscous with toasted pine nuts

1 Heat oil in a large nonstick skillet over medium heat.
Add yellow squash and zucchini and cook, stirring occasionally, 5 minutes or until lightly browned.

2 Add remaining ingredients except couscous; stir to
mix. Bring to a boil, reduce heat, cover skillet and simmer
5 minutes to blend flavors.

3 Uncover and simmer 8 to 10 minutes longer until liquid is reduced slightly.

4 Meanwhile prepare couscous as box directs.

5 Serve chickpea mixture over couscous.

TIME: 30 min

SERVES 4

PER SERVING: 431 cal,
  13 g pro, 66 g car, 8 g fiber,
  14 g fat (2 g saturated fat),
  0 mg chol, 1,809 mg sod

TIP *Pitted marinated Greek
kalamata olives are available in jars.*

TIME: 50 min

SERVES 4

PER SERVING: 563 cal,
  29 g pro, 65 g car, 8 g fiber,
  23 g fat (12 g saturated fat),
  61 mg chol, 1,591 mg sod

TIP *Save money by buying cheese in chunks or blocks and shredding it yourself.*

Cheese and Vegetable Chowder

3 strips (3 oz) bacon
1 cup chopped onion
2 chicken-broth cubes
3 cups cubed, scrubbed all-purpose potatoes
1 cup diced carrots
1 can (15 oz) whole-kernel corn, drained
1 box (10 oz) frozen chopped kale or spinach
4 cups (1 qt) 1% lowfat milk
1/4 cup plus 2 Tbsp all-purpose flour
3/4 tsp salt
6 oz Cheddar cheese, shredded (1 1/2 cups; see Tip)
GARNISH: sliced scallions

1 Cook bacon in a 5-qt pot over medium heat until crisp. Drain on paper towel, then crumble. Discard all but 2 tsp fat from pot.

2 Sauté onion in fat in pot over medium heat 4 to 5 minutes, stirring often, until tender. Stir in 2 cups water, the broth cubes, potatoes, carrots, corn and kale. Bring to a boil, reduce heat, cover and, stirring often to break up frozen kale, simmer 15 minutes or until vegetables are tender.

3 Whisk milk, flour and salt in a medium bowl until blended. Stir into pot. Bring to a gentle boil, stirring occasionally, and cook 3 minutes or until slightly thickened.

4 Add cheese; stir until melted. Ladle into soup plates or bowls. Sprinkle servings with bacon; garnish with scallions.

TIME: 1 hr 50 min

SERVES 6

PER SERVING: 346 cal,
  16 g pro, 26 g car, 5 g fiber,
  22 g fat (7 g saturated fat),
  27 mg chol, 1,451 mg sod

TIP To keep foil from sticking
to the cheese, use nonstick
foil or coat foil with nonstick spray.

Eggplant Parmigiana

2 eggplants (2 1/2 lb), cut in 1/2-in.-thick rounds
1/4 cup olive oil
3/4 tsp salt
1/2 tsp pepper
1 jar (26 oz) marinara sauce
1 1/2 cups (6 oz) shredded part-skim mozzarella cheese
1 cup grated Parmesan cheese
GARNISH: chopped parsley

1 Remove broiler pan with rack from oven. Have a
shallow 2 1/2-qt baking dish ready.

2 Broiling eggplant in 2 batches, layer 1/2 on broiler
rack and brush with 1/2 the oil; sprinkle with 1/2 the salt
and pepper. Broil 4 in. from heat 6 to 8 minutes per side
until lightly browned and tender. Repeat with rest.

3 Spread 1/2 cup marinara sauce in baking dish. Line
with half the eggplant. Spoon on 1 1/4 cups sauce; top with
1 cup mozzarella, then remaining eggplant, sauce and mozzarella. Sprinkle with Parmesan; cover with foil (see Tip).

4 Bake 45 minutes or until bubbly. Let rest 15 minutes.
Garnish and serve.

Index

(Page numbers in *italic* refer to illustrations.)

Photo credits

Cover: Sang An; pp. 8, 11, 12: Mark Thomas; p. 15: Alison Miksch; p. 16: Mark Thomas; p. 19: Alison Miksch; p. 20: Jacqueline Hopkins; p. 23: Sang An; p. 24: John Uher; p. 27: Jacqueline Hopkins; p. 28: Charles Schiller, pp. 31, 32, 35: John Uher; p. 36: Mark Thomas; p. 39: John Uher; p. 40: Mark Thomas; pp. 43, 44: Charles Schiller; p. 47: Mark Thomas; p. 49: Alison Miksch; p. 50: Mark Thomas; pp. 52, 55: Alison Miksch; p. 56: Jacqueline Hopkins; p. 59: John Uher; p. 60: Jacqueline Hopkins; pp. 63, 64: John Uher; p. 67: Sang An; pp. 68, 71, 72: Charles Schiller; p. 75: John Uher; p. 76: Charles Schiller; pp. 79, 80: Mark Thomas; p. 83: John Uher; pp. 84, 87: Sang An; pp. 88, 91: John Uher; p. 92: Sang An; p. 95: Charles Schiller; p. 96: Jacqueline Hopkins; p. 99: John Uher; p. 100: Charles Schiller; pp. 102, 105: John Uher; p. 106: Mark Thomas; p. 109: Alison Miksch; p. 110: John Uher; p. 113: Sang An; p. 114: Marcus Tullis; p. 117: Jacqueline Hopkins; pp. 118, 121, 123: Charles Schiller. Back cover (clockwise from top left): Charles Schiller, Mark Thomas, Jacqueline Hopkins, Marcus Tullis.

Acknowledgments

The publisher wishes to thank Jane Chesnutt; Ellen R. Greene, Nancy Dell'Aria, Mary-Ellen Banashek, Marisol Vera, Terry Grieco Kenny, Christine Makuch and Susan Kadel; Sue Kakstys, Michele Fedele, Robb Riedel, Kim Walker, Greg Robertson, Margaret Farley; Cathy Dorsey; and all the photographers whose images are reproduced in the book.

Recipes and food styling by Nancy Dell'Aria, Terry Grieco Kenny, Christine Makuch and Susan Kadel.